ALGONQUIN PARK

ALGONQUIN PARK

A PHOTOGRAPHIC JOURNEY

IAIN MCNAB

NIMBUS
PUBLISHING

Nimbus Publishing Limited
3731 Mackintosh St, Halifax, NS B3K 5A5
(902) 455-4286 nimbus.ca

Printed and bound in Canada

NB1315

Design: Jenn Embree

Library and Archives Canada Cataloguing in Publication

McNab, Iain, photographer, writer of introduction
Algonquin Park : a photographic journey / Iain McNab.

ISBN 978-1-77108-571-7 (softcover)

1. Algonquin Provincial Park (Ont.)—Pictorial works. I. Title.

FC3065.A65M36 2018   971.3'147   C2017-907953-0

Nimbus Publishing acknowledges the financial support for its publishing activities from the Government of Canada, the Canada Council for the Arts, and from the Province of Nova Scotia. We are pleased to work in partnership with the Province of Nova Scotia to develop and promote our creative industries for the benefit of all Nova Scotians.

In memory of
CATHERINE BORTHWICK MCNAB
Greenock, Scotland
1938-1986

Wife, mother, sister, daughter

Your presence we miss
Your memory we treasure
Loving you always
Forgetting you never

FOREWORD

ALGONQUIN PARK HAS ALWAYS BEEN special to me. It has been a large part of my life since I arrived as a seventeen-year-old junior forest ranger in June 1948. When the program ended in August of that year, I was hired as a forest ranger. Part of the job requirement at the time was the ability to handle a canoe in rough water. Since I had spent my early years on an island in Lake Temagami where canoes, boats, and dog teams were part of everyday life, this was not a problem.

I worked and lived in the park for the next eighteen years. Because of the variety of jobs, I looked forward to going to work every day. The Department of Lands and Forests maintained the telephone systems to communicate between the fire towers and Chief Ranger Office. Lines had to be checked and repaired, and batteries replaced in the tower telephones. I fought forest fires, and searched for lost people. We maintained the portages, campsites, docks, and tower man's cabins. I scaled logs in the lumber camps in the winter. Since there was no electricity, we cut ice for the ice houses and five hundred cords of wood for the stoves and furnaces in all the buildings. I worked with Fisheries Research on the spawning beds, and assisted game wardens in catching poachers. Best of all were the great people I met and worked with.

Being outdoors most of the time, I witnessed nature at its best. I've seen northern lights so bright you didn't need headlights to drive. Snowshoeing across Cache Lake one cold clear night with a full moon so bright it reflected off the pure white snow, creating a three-foot-wide diamond-studded streak beginning at my feet and ending part way across

Witnessing the northern lights is a special treat at Algonquin Park, where there are no tall buildings or city lights to lessen the spectacle. The northern lights are caused by collisions between gaseous particles in the Earth's atmosphere and charged particles released from the sun's atmosphere. They vary in colour depending on the type of particles colliding.

the lake. It stayed with me until I got off the lake. From my front window on Clarke Lake, I counted fourteen wolves on the ice, and heard them howling frequently. I've witnessed a deer giving birth.

From a department aircraft, a fire tower, or a trail lookout, you get a sense of the vastness of the wilderness. The autumn colours are spectacular. Each season has a beauty all its own. Algonquin was a wonderful place to work. I continue to visit every year—to hike, canoe, fish, and camp.

After thirty-six years, I retired in 1984. In 1989, the Friends of Algonquin Park asked me to co-ordinate and supervise the building of the new logging museum. I was delighted to accept the offer. It was a grand finale to my Algonquin experiences.

Seventy years later, we still spend most of the summer camping in the park. The beautiful photos in this book bring back so many memories of this wonderful, special place that is Algonquin Park.

TOM LINKLATER

INTRODUCTION

I MADE MY FIRST VISIT TO ALGONQUIN Park in the summer of 1993. A ten-day trip, where I camped at Mew Lake Campground with my wife (then girlfriend) and her brother Simon and his young family. Within a few days we were hooked— ten days was not long enough. The wildlife alone was amazing: moose and bear sightings on our first trip when many people never see any.

The next time I went to the park was in the fall of 1997 after purchasing a small trailer. I took many pictures on that trip; the trees in all their fall colours were stunning. I saw moose again and tried my best to capture their beauty. My camera was a small 35mm point-and-shoot, but unfortunately I was not getting the images that I was seeing in real life. The moose were not close enough in these shots—I am not sure you would even have known there was a moose in the photos.

I was not discouraged, and in the following twenty years, I have spent countless hours chasing moose, foxes, bears, and the perfect shot. I have upgraded my camera gear numerous times, worked on my technical skills, and formed friendships with other photographers in the park.

Algonquin, which was established in 1893, is a multi-faceted and rewarding subject. It is a sprawling 7,700 square kilometres in size and contains over two thousand lakes, one thousand species of plants, as well as birds, fish, and mammals. Located 300 kilometres north of Toronto, it has camping and

The photographer, shooting in this blind, tries to blend into nature with camouflage clothing and camera gear. Photo credit Shea McNab.

fishing, hiking, or canoe tripping. Picnicking and swimming in the warmer months or cross-country skiing or snowshoeing in the winter.

In this rich and dynamic environment, photography is a constant. Whether they are using a cellphone, i-Pad, point-and-shoot, or DSLR, someone is always taking photographs.

It wasn't until 2001, after my son Conor was born, that I purchased my first 35mm single-lens reflex (SLR) camera. It was a Canon Rebel G. I took many rolls of film and slides with this camera on numerous interior canoe and camping trips in Algonquin Park. I was sure that I would have no problem capturing all those images I was seeing with my eyes. That was not the case, and I

realized I needed to learn how to use my camera properly. I started by taking a camera class, joining The Cambridge Camera Club and reading many books and magazines. My pictures were still not book-worthy but my interest in learning became a great focus for me.

In 2004, I purchased my first digital camera. It was a Canon PowerShot. It was nice to be able to see my photos right away and not have to wait for the film to be developed, but I still was not happy with the quality of my images.

In 2007, I purchased my first DSLR (digital single-lens reflex) camera, a Canon Rebel XT. This I kept for a short time and soon traded up to a Canon EOS 30D. With this camera I was starting to see better photos. It was very user-friendly, and I started enjoying the photos I was getting.

I spent a lot of time in Algonquin Park with these cameras—shooting and practising. Every year since my son was born, a minimum of two weeks every summer was spent camping along Highway 60 in Algonquin Park. I was able to find much wildlife to photograph, whether driving through the park or hiking one of the many trails.

In 2008, I started to photograph weddings to improve my technique, but eventually decided this was not the way I wanted to move forward; I kept going back to nature.

In 2009, I upgraded to a full-frame DSLR Canon 5D. I was getting a better-quality photo with this. In 2013, I upgraded again from the Canon 5D to the Canon 5D Mark III. Shortly after purchasing this, I decided that I had no longer any need for my studio lighting and thought the money from selling that equipment could go towards the purchase of a 400mm lens. This would get me closer to the animals I wanted to photograph.

In the summer of 2014, I was shooting pictures of the black bears that frequent the blueberry patch at Mew Lake in Algonquin Park. The bears tend to roam around, and I was constantly moving to a better position. Upon moving to yet another spot I came across another fellow who was also shooting photos of the bears. I paused, so as not to interrupt him. He looked away from his camera and gave me a nod. He then said, "Come on over." We started taking photos side by side and got to chatting. He told me he was from Minden, Ontario, about an hour's drive from Algonquin Park. It was at this time that something clicked. I was sure I knew this fellow. I looked at him and said "pondrader"? He smiled and said "yes." As fate would have it, Jeff Manser and I had chatted many times previously and commented on each other's photos online. We are both members on a photo website called "Photography on The Net" or POTN. Since that

(TOP) *A grey jay, or whisky jack, poses on top of a camera, proving a delightful distraction.*

(BOTTOM) *A fearless grey jay eats cashews from Kent Nonomura's hand during a photo outing.*

day in Algonquin Park we have been in touch with each other, pretty much on a daily basis.

We made plans to meet up in Algonquin in October and spent a few days camping at Lake of Two Rivers campground. On my last day, we hiked out to March Hare Lake, which you can get to by hiking the Mizzy Lake Trail. It was on this day that I first met Kent Nonomura, another photographer. Kent is from Brampton, Ontario, which is

Photo friends Kent Nonomura and Jeff Manser shoot a female moose crossing the road. It takes practice and good luck to get a great moose shot.

only about forty-five minutes from where I live in Cambridge. It wasn't long before Kent and I began meeting up on weekends to take in some photography. The almost daily correspondence between Jeff and me soon included Kent.

I would have to say that my photography has improved a great deal since meeting Jeff and Kent. I have received a lot of good critique, comments, and some criticism from them, and they have received the same from me. Now when I make a trip to Algonquin, I usually meet up with one or both of them.

It was Jeff who first suggested to me that the full-frame 5D Mark III was not really suited for wildlife photography. (It was more of a portrait and wedding camera.) I was constantly cropping photos, even with a 400mm lens. His suggestion

was a Canon 7D Mark II. After a few months, I decided to make the change. The 7D Mark II has a 1.6x crop sensor and ten-frames-per-second shutter. The speed is great for capturing birds in flight and for getting the action shots that I was missing out on with the Mark III.

In late 2016, I purchased the Canon EF100-400 Mark II lens. I still have the EF400mm F 5.6 prime that I started with. However, my daughter, Shea, uses it now. So that is my current set-up, and I use this whenever I go out to photograph—the Canon 7D Mark II and EF 100-400 Mark II. A lot of the images in this book are from this camera set-up.

When I started taking the 35mm SLR to the park, it was mostly for fishing trips in the spring with my brother-in-law Paul Stewart. As we would sit by the campfire at night, the conversations were

The office at Canoe Lake where visitors can obtain day or overnight permits for the park, which was founded in 1893.

mostly about photography. Discussions about types of film, aperture, and shutter speeds, camera brands, and lenses. Little did I realize at the time, he would be a big influence in my photography journey.

We are all digital now, but we use different brands of gear. Paul is a Nikon shooter. As with all my friends who shoot Nikon, we make fun of each other about our chosen brands. But it is all in fun. All the big-name manufacturers have great equipment. They each have gear that is excellent for whatever application you need, depending on your style of photography.

As for me shooting Canon, it was simply the brand I chose at the time I purchased my 35mm camera. Obviously gear is expensive to purchase, so usually most people stick to the brand they

started their lens collection with. New camera bodies are released all the time, but it is your glass that is important, not the camera body. Once you have spent a bit of money on lenses, it is quite costly to switch brands and rebuild your lens lineup. I have many times over the years contemplated switching brands, but the cost factor has kept me with Canon. I do, however, prefer the images that I get from my Canon, colours, bokeh (the aesthetic quality of the out-of-focus areas), etc. Definitely a personal choice.

I have been asked many times, by many people wanting to get into photography, what they should buy. My question back to them always is: what do you want to take pictures of?

After it is all said and done, it is the person behind the viewfinder making the image, not the

A spectacular sunrise over Lake of Two Rivers provides haunting smoky reflections on the water.

gear. It does not require the most expensive camera and lenses.

For the most part these days I am a lone shooter. Don't get me wrong. It is always enjoyable to get out with someone else who enjoys shooting photos, but many times I have missed opportunities when I am having a conversation with someone. I am also an early bird. I enjoy getting out when nobody else is around. It is quiet, the wildlife is more active, and the light in the early morning is much softer than mid day when the sun is directly over you. I always try to get the sun at my back. An animal shot with the sun behind me is my preference. With that being said, I won't pass up the opportunity for a sunrise shot either. So turn around! Think outside the box. I try to say to myself: get a different angle, a different composition. What can I do to get something different than what others are getting? It is easy to just point and shoot or set up my tripod and shoot. It is trying to be creative that is the hard part. What angle? Get lower to the ground? What aperture should I use? What shutter speed?

When I am out with someone else, like Brian Kenkel (my usual local shooting partner), Kent, or Jeff, we usually take off in different directions. I have been in the airfield at Algonquin Provincial Park at least a kilometre from them. When one of us comes across something of interest, we text each other.

Photography is my therapy, my Happy Place. I don't need to think about work, paying bills, driving one child here and the other there, working on the house or doing laundry. I can enjoy the moment and take it home. Put me in Algonquin Park and it just gets better. The cool morning air, the silence, the sound the wind makes blowing through the trees. Hearing the sound of the birds and frogs in the swamps, or the odd grunt of a moose. Feeling the warmth of the sun when it hits me, or when it burns off the fog or darkness. It is pure pleasure, plain and simple.

I could not have gotten to this point in my life without my wife, Alison, and for that I thank you. For her giving me a home, not just a house, for my children, Conor and Shea. All of you for putting up with me setting the alarm for 1 or 2 A.M. so I can head for the park to capture the sunrise, while dragging you all along.

Nor could I have achieved the level that I am at with my photography without the guidance and companionship from Paul Stewart, Jeff Manser, Kent Nonomura, and Brian Kenkel. I am always listening to what you say, even if sometimes I appear not to be. You guys keep my life interesting. I am currently sitting at my computer desk in the basement writing this while doing the laundry. I think it is time to run upstairs and set my alarm for 1 A.M. to head to Algonquin.

If you see me there on the trails, don't be afraid to say "Hi!"

I am still after my perfect shot.

IAÎN MCNAB

Alison, the photographer's wife, takes a break along Booth's Rock Trail, Rock Lake.

A red fox kit appears both shy and vulnerable in this photo. Algonquin Park is home to fifty-five species of mammals, but the foxes, it could be argued, may be the cutest.

(BELOW) *In this fantastic view from Booth's Rock Trail, Rock Lake, trees form a dense and irregular frame for the water while white clouds gently float overhead.*

(FACING TOP) *The Algonquin sign at the East Gate, Highway 60, welcomes visitors to the vast park, which is larger than Prince Edward Island.*

(FACING BOTTOM) *A sturdy yurt at Mew Lake provides shelter from the elements.*

(OVERLEAF) *Dramatic storm clouds loom over Costello Lake, threatening to disrupt the smooth placid surface. Algonquin Park's 2,400 lakes make it popular for swimming and canoe tripping.*

(ABOVE) *A red-tailed hawk visits the photographer's campsite at Lake of Two Rivers.*

(BOTTOM) *A daisy, captured on its own along the trail at the Logging Museum, is beautiful in its simplicity.*

(FACING) *This innovative shot at Big Pines Trail shows a different photographic perspective.*

(ABOVE) *A funky cedar tree along the shore of Lake of Two Rivers shows how a simple subject can become an intriguing shot.*

(FACING) *This spruce bog is filled with lily pads, but is also home to wildlife which prefer low-lying wet areas such as bogs, ponds, and beaver meadows.*

(OVERLEAF) *In the spring, Costello Creek feels fresh and crisp. The park's personality changes with the seasons, with each one showing a different type of beauty.*

(TOP) *A small dragonfly at Rock Lake provides a gorgeous slice of colour in nature. The park has over seven thousand species of insects.*

(BOTTOM) *This black bear on Highway 60 seems oblivious to the photographer, who was lucky enough to spot a bear on his very first visit to Algonquin, whetting his appetite for more.*

(FACING) *Storm clouds from the visitors' centre feel ominous.*

(OVERLEAF) *Coming across a bull moose like this in the water reminds the photographer of the animal's tremendous size. Male moose typically weigh over five hundred kilograms, the females less.*

(ABOVE) *A snowshoe hare is brave enough to snack at the photographer's campsite at Mew Lake.*

(FACING TOP) *A graceful deer is captured eating breakfast on Highway 60. Early morning may be the best time to see most birds and mammals up close in the park.*

(BOTTOM) *In this summertime view from Opeongo Lookout, you can feel the park's warmth and contentment.*

(OVERLEAF) *At sunrise, Smoke Lake takes on a mysterious air, the water dark and unreadable. Algonquin Park was immortalized by iconic Canadian artist Tom Thomson, who attained international recognition with his paintings of scenes of this beauty.*

A loon taking flight on Mew Lake creates splashes of water captured in this shot.

(ABOVE) *Curious fox kits watch every move the photographer makes.*

(FACING) *A handsome red fox checks out the photographer. The animals, while shy by nature, sometimes approach humans.*

(FACING) *The park plane takes off to do some patrolling on Smoke Lake.*

(BELOW) *A monarch butterfly is stunning in this blueberry patch, its colours sharp and vivid.*

(OVERLEAF) *Vegetation peeks through the water in this shoreline view along Rock Lake.*

(RIGHT) *One of many portage signs along Highway 60 giving visitors directions. According to a recent newspaper story, the park gets one hundred thousand campground visits each year and three times as many backcountry visits.*

(BELOW) *Paddling on Cache Lake.*

(FACING) *A lone canoeist paddles on Rock Lake, undaunted. The only way to explore the interior of the park is by canoe or on foot.*

(TOP) *A female moose has a snack on a pond, surrounded by bugs. Females typically weigh over four hundred kilograms.*

(BOTTOM) *A great blue heron is on the hunt for a meal.*

(FACING) *The moon creates a splendid nighttime scene at Mew Lake.*

(OVERLEAF) *Interesting light after a storm at Brewer Lake creates a mystical, magical vibe.*

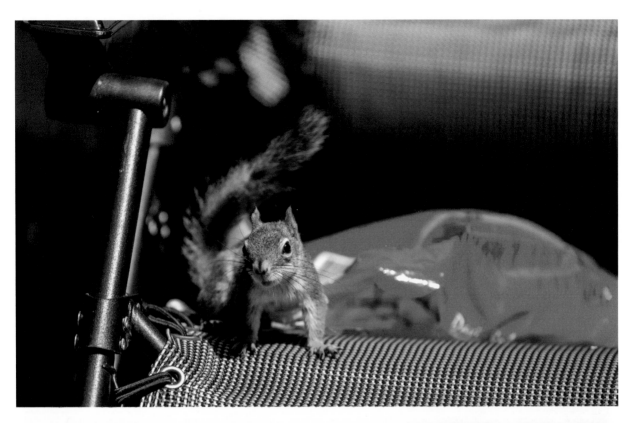

(TOP) *A spunky red squirrel looks for peanuts on the photographer's lawn chair.*

(BOTTOM) *Visitors are shown getting ready for the water taxi at Opeongo Lake, the park's largest lake.*

(FACING) *Indian pipe, a spiky and unusual looking plant, is common along Highway 60.*

(OVERLEAF) *A loon carries a chick on its back in this adorable photo.*

(ABOVE) *The photographer's daughter, Shea, enjoying the moment at a favourite spot, Smoke Lake, Highway 60.*

(FACING) *A lookout over the Beaver Pond Trail shows a densely vegetated scene.*

(OVERLEAF) *Fog burning away from the sunshine creates interesting light on Opeongo Road. Colours merge and complement each other.*

(ABOVE) *A red fox poses with a bit of a squint.*

(FACING TOP) *A water lily on Cache Lake is perfect in its singular, simple beauty.*

(FACING BOTTOM) *Lilies form a lovely covering for this lake.*

(ABOVE) *This photo shows the interior of a camboose shanty at the Logging Museum Trail. The winter lumber camps typically had a central fire with a large chimney. Men often slept fully clothed due to the cold.*

(FACING) *A log chute on the Logging Museum Trail helps educate visitors about the park's past. Visitors can learn about Algonquin Park's logging history from the 1830s to the present.*

(OVERLEAF) *There are so many lakes in Algonquin Park that it would take a lifetime to see them all. On this sunny day, Jack Lake appears languid and undisturbed, with fallen trees slowly decomposing on the water's edge.*

Dark clouds on the Lookout Trail show another face of Algonquin Park, which, in 2017, marked the one-hundred-year anniversary of Tom Thomson's untimely death. The artist's upturned canoe was found on Canoe Lake, and his body eight days later. From 1912 to 1917, Thomson created hundreds of striking paintings of the park, which gave him solitude and inspiration. His death was surrounded by mystery.

The photographer's son, Conor, hikes along this undulating logging road in the fall. The trees have changed colour, but it is still warm enough to go without a coat.

(ABOVE) *Pileated woodpeckers are the largest woodpeckers in Algonquin.*

(FACING) *Ragged Falls in the fall, with the water framed by brightly coloured leaves.*

(OVERLEAF) *Spectacular fall leaves on Costello Lake create a blur of colour on the water surface.*

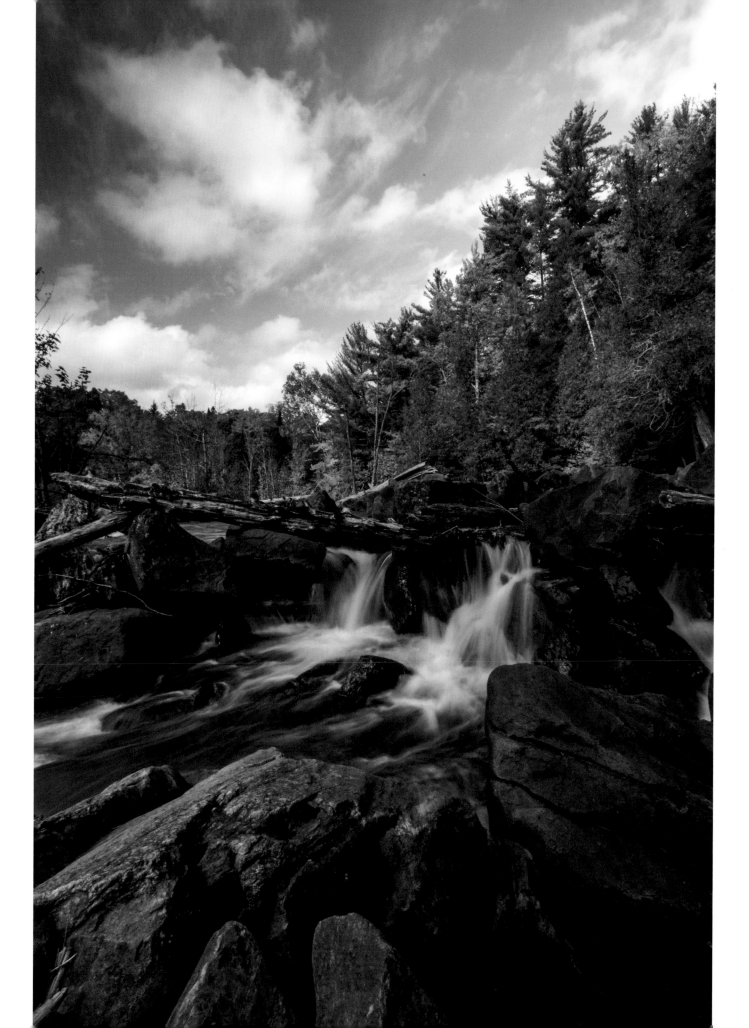

(TOP) *A typical interior campsite on Opeongo Lake is both private and exhilarating.*

(BOTTOM) *Sunrise over the bog at Highway 60 feels lazy and serene.*

(FACING) *Fall colours along Mizzy Lake Trail add spark.*

(ABOVE) *A bull moose in the fall gives the photographer a complacent look, confident in his size advantage.*

(FACING TOP) *A spiderweb with early morning condensation looks like a work of art.*

(FACING BOTTOM) *A black-and-white spiderweb with early morning condensation is shot up close.*

Maple leaves show their rich fall colours on Highway 60. Algonquin contains one thousand species of plants as well as common trees like the maple.

A loon swims across Mew Lake in the early morning light, leaving a subtle wake.

(BELOW) *A cloudy fall day at Mizzy Lake Trail hints at cooler temperatures and new beginnings.*

(ABOVE) *A healthy looking red fox poses for the photographer. Foxes, bears, moose, and deer are some of the favourite photo subjects in the park.*

(OVERLEAF) *This fall shot from the Secret Opeongo Lookout reflects the vast size of the park.*

Fall colours on Booth's Rock Trail merge into a red, yellow, and orange tapestry.

Sunrise from the dock at Cache Lake is moody and still.

A grey jay is captured taking flight. The curious birds eat just about anything, from berries to small animals, hoarding food in summer to ensure their winter survival.

A grey jay, or whisky jack, is photographed against a backdrop of fall colours.

(OVERLEAF) *In this close-up of trees, the fall colours on Highway 60 are perfectly composed, as though by an artist's brush.*

Lake of Two Rivers Point in the fall is rugged.

A foggy sunrise in the old airfield at Mew Lake creates an unusual ambience.

(ABOVE) *An American bittern searches for dinner at Wolf Howl Pond. The cleverly camouflaged heron can be difficult to spot in marshes due to its colouring.*

(FACING) *Leaves on the ground along a trail at Highway 60 create a slippery carpet of colour.*

(ABOVE) *Driftwood at Rock Lake provides a stark contrast to the colorful fall leaves.*

(FACING) *This little pine tree at Found Lake is popular with photographers.*

(ABOVE) *A sunrise on Costello Lake creates an ominous palette of reds and blacks, making it hard to tell where the water starts and ends.*

(FACING) *A cloudy fall day at Mizzy Lake Trail shows the park's gloomier side.*

(ABOVE) *At sunrise from Highway 60, Mew Lake is an explosion of silhouettes and colour.*

(FACING) *Canoes are always parked on the beach at Lake of Two Rivers ready to be used.*

(OVERLEAF) *In the fall, the view from the Secret Lookout Trail is a kaleidoscope of colour.*

Fall colours at Tea Lake feel fresh and crisp.

(ABOVE) *This view of Rock Lake in the fall at Booth's Rock Trail is exhilarating.*

(OVERLEAF) *The smooth, glassy water at Lake of Two Rivers at sunrise takes on surprising colour.*

(RIGHT) *The old truck at Algonquin Outfitters at Oxtongue Lake.*

(BOTTOM) *One of the old logging trucks at the Logging Museum is a reminder of the park's forestry past. Visitors can enjoy a video presentation as well as displays such as a recreated camboose camp and an amphibious tug called an "alligator."*

One of Algonquin Outfitters's canoe rental fleet is shown on the water.

Fall colours on Highway 60 are cheeful and bright.

Sunrise on Smoke Creek produces a delicate mix of yellows and greens.

The photographer captured these fall colours on Highway 60 while on an outing with shooting buddy Kent Nonomura.

(BELOW) *Along Smoke Creek in the fall, the water appears cool and the trees hot with pigment.*

(OVERLEAF) *Stars over Opeongo Lake illuminate the park's beauty at night. They feel both delicate and bright.*

(ABOVE) *A female moose in the fall on Highway 60 seems unconcerned by people.*

(FACING TOP) *The crest of a hill and fall colours on Highway 60 feel busy.*

(FACING BOTTOM) *Fall colours along Smoke Creek, where humans can commune with nature.*

(ABOVE) *A dock with a chair at sunrise on Smoke Lake creates an enigmatic and gorgeous scene.*

(FACING) *Maple leaves in the fall on Highway 60 are in the final stages of red.*

(ABOVE) *The sunrise on Smoke Lake feels cool and clean.*

(FACING TOP) *An old alligator boat on the Logging Museum Trail provides another glimpse into the past.*

(FACING BOTTOM) *Fall colours in a swamp on Highway 60 add an odd reflection.*

(OVERLEAF) A *black bear cub makes itself seen in a blueberry patch. Visitors to the park are advised to take binoculars to make spotting easier; they are also advised to keep a respectful distance from animals like this.*

(TOP) *Canoes on the beach at sunrise in Lake of Two Rivers seem as restful as the water.*

(BOTTOM) *A loon and chick create a charming silhouette. It has been said that the call of the loon can be heard from every campground in the park.*

(FACING) *Fall colours on Arowhon Road are intense and vibrant.*

Sunset on March Hare Lake, one of many lakes visited each year.

From time to time, photographers come across artists in the park painting, this one at Smoke Lake. Some may still be inspired by Tom Thomson, who, one hundred years ago, shared his passion for the park with fellow artists who then formed the Group of Seven. Thomson's dstinctive palette and brushwork made his paintings easily recognized.

(ABOVE) *These cool log-cabin signposts have been appearing in the park over the last two years.*

(FACING) *A Opeongo Outfitters canoe at Rock Lake Beach is ready for use.*

(ABOVE) *A campground chipmunk is looking for peanuts. Chipmunks eat seasonally, with their diet changing according to the availability of food. In the summer, they put food in small caches spread throughout their territory.*

(FACING) *Looking down Ragged Falls in November, the view is powerful and stark.*

(OVERLEAF) *Fog burning away from the sunshine creates glorious light on Opeongo Road.*

(ABOVE) *A female moose takes a rest at Mew Lake.*

(FACING) *This sunrise on Lake of Two Rivers is cool and hot at the same time.*

(OVERLEAF) *This Mew Lake sunrise on Highway 60 is enchanted.*

(ABOVE) *Photographer's daughter, Shea, takes a rest while snowshoeing, another popular park activity.*

(BOTTOM) *The start of winter in November at Spruce Bog Trail, with frost covering the wooden boards, a time for some of the park's animals to hibernate.*

(FACING) *A stand of birch trees, Highway 60. Trees are clearly the largest living things in the park and some visitors become adept at identifying the many types.*

(ABOVE) *A few cross-country skiers at Mew Lake.*

(FACING) *Snow makes hiking more difficult but no less rewarding.*

A pine marten in winter. The animals are similar in size to a mink with a long luxurious tail adding length. In winter, they are known to burrow into tree roots to protect themselves from the cold.

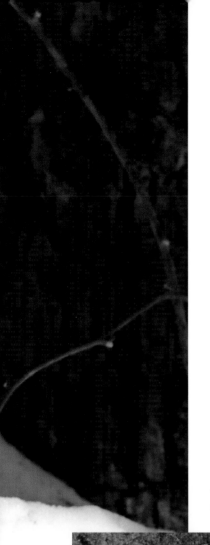

A pine marten on a tree branch. The cuddly looking creature with the cute black nose is actually an adept hunter and a carnivore.

(BELOW) *Not every morning has a beautiful sunrise. On this morning, the sun only appeared for a few minutes over the old airfield at Mew Lake, and then disappeared for the day, failing to warm the chilly landscape.*

(FACING TOP) *The photographer's daughter, Shea, braves minus 30 degrees Celsius in February for sunrise shots.*

(FACING BOTTOM) *A crow visits the photographer's campsite at Mew Lake.*

(ABOVE) *Smoke Lake sunrise in the winter, when some animals adapt by reducing their body temperatures and becoming inactive.*

(FACING) *A winter sunrise on Highway 60 adds warmth to a frigid blue scene.*

(OVERLEAF) *A boathouse on Smoke Lake is locked in ice.*

This papa fox relaxes.